A Crabtree

Let's Go Fish

FRESHWATER FISHING

By Kerri Mazzarella

CRABTREE
Publishing Company
www.crabtreebooks.com

School-to-Home Support for Caregivers and Teachers

This high-interest book is designed to motivate striving students with engaging topics while building fluency, vocabulary, and an interest in reading. Here are a few questions and activities to help the reader build upon his or her comprehension skills.

Before Reading:

- *What do I think this book is about?*
- *What do I know about this topic?*
- *What do I want to learn about this topic?*
- *Why am I reading this book?*

During Reading:

- *I wonder why...*
- *I'm curious to know...*
- *How is this like something I already know?*
- *What have I learned so far?*

After Reading:

- *What was the author trying to teach me?*
- *What are some details?*
- *How did the photographs and captions help me understand more?*
- *Read the book again and look for the vocabulary words.*
- *What questions do I still have?*

Extension Activities:

- *What was your favorite part of the book? Write a paragraph on it.*
- *Draw a picture of your favorite thing you learned from the book.*

TABLE OF CONTENTS

WHERE TO FISH

Fishing is an activity that is enjoyed by **anglers** all over the world. Freshwater fishing is one type of fishing. It takes place in bodies of fresh water and can be done on land or by boat.

Ponds, lakes, and rivers are all great locations to freshwater fish. They are easy to find and are filled with different types of freshwater fish.

Fresh water is water that you can drink. It does not contain salt, unlike the ocean which contains a lot of salt.

People fish for many reasons. Some people fish to provide food for their family, some fish to earn a living, and some fish as a sport or hobby.

FUN FACTS

Aquaculture is the practice of raising and breeding fish in a controlled environment. Fish farms are responsible for producing freshwater fish such as catfish, salmon, and trout.

Freshwater fish can be found throughout North America. Young and old people alike seek the thrill of catching fish. It's never too late to learn how to fish.

TYPES OF FISH

Many different freshwater fish are caught each year. There are over 800 **species** of freshwater fish that live in North America.

carp

pike

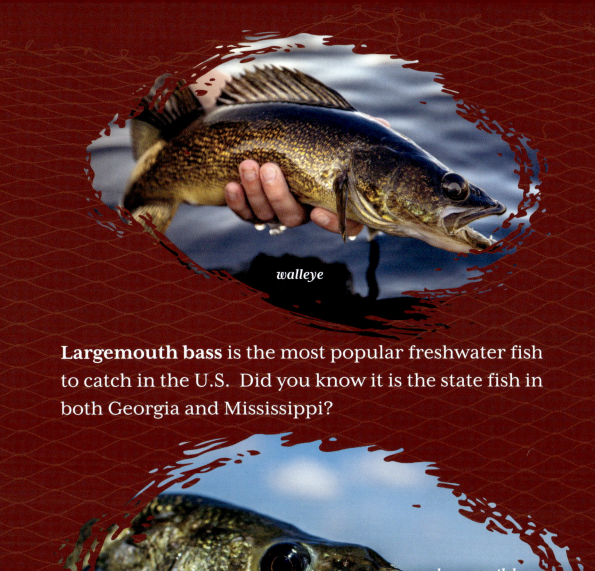

walleye

Largemouth bass is the most popular freshwater fish to catch in the U.S. Did you know it is the state fish in both Georgia and Mississippi?

largemouth bass

Some other common freshwater fish include smallmouth bass, crappie, catfish, and walleye. Some freshwater fish are caught just for fun, and others are kept because they are good to eat!

catfish

FUN FACTS
Salmon is the number one consumed fish by people living in the U.S. and Canada.

Salmon are **anadromous** which means they live in both fresh water and salt water. They are born in fresh water then **migrate** to the sea. They return to fresh water to reproduce.

SAFETY AND RULES

Safety should always come first while fishing. A life vest should be worn while fishing on a boat. It is also important to have a first aid kit on hand.

Always remember to handle fish carefully. Some fish have sharp fins that can pierce your skin. Use caution when casting your hook and be aware of your surroundings.

Did you know fishing hook injuries happen often? You wouldn't want to hook yourself or a friend, would you?

Every state has rules for freshwater fishing. Unless you are on private property, you will need to purchase a freshwater fishing **license**.

The average U.S. cost of an annual fishing license for residents is $25 and $61 for non-residents.

There are seasons when freshwater fish are permitted to be caught and kept. It is important to know the size limits of any fish you are planning to keep. Don't forget to bring your tape measure.

RODS AND EQUIPMENT

Special equipment is used for freshwater fishing. There are thousands of different rod and reel combinations to choose from.

Some rods come as a combo which includes a rod and reel. Other more expensive rods and reels can be purchased separately.

The average cost of a rod and reel combo with line is about $80.

The most common fishing rods are made of **fiberglass**. It is important to choose one that is stiff enough not to break when you catch a fish, but flexible enough so your line does not snap when you catch a big fish.

Some rod combos come with fishing line. More experienced anglers like to purchase special line. Monofilament or "mono" is the most common fishing line used. It comes in different strengths and colors.

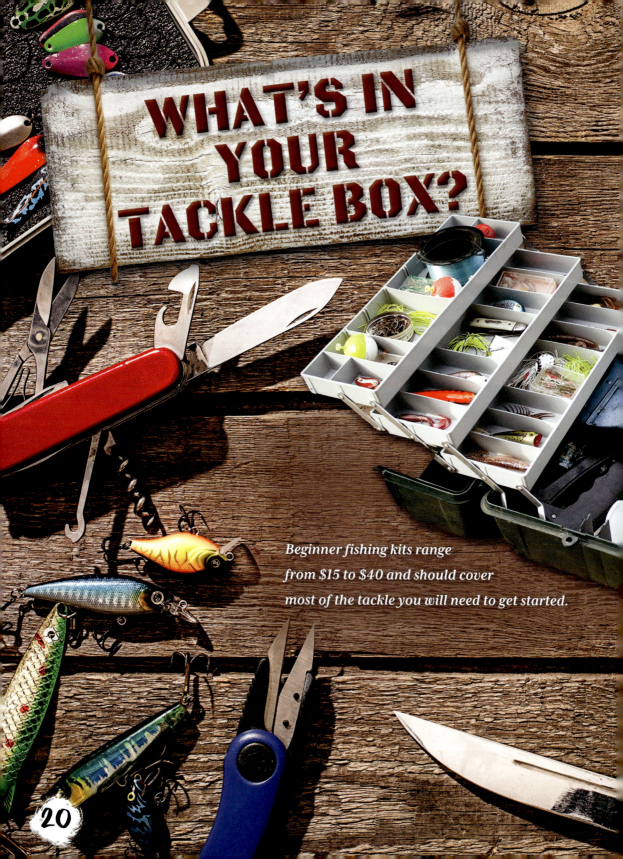

WHAT'S IN YOUR TACKLE BOX?

Beginner fishing kits range from $15 to $40 and should cover most of the tackle you will need to get started.

Most anglers have a **tackle** box. It should include things such as bobbers, weights, hooks, extra line, knives, leader, swivels, pliers, and **lures**.

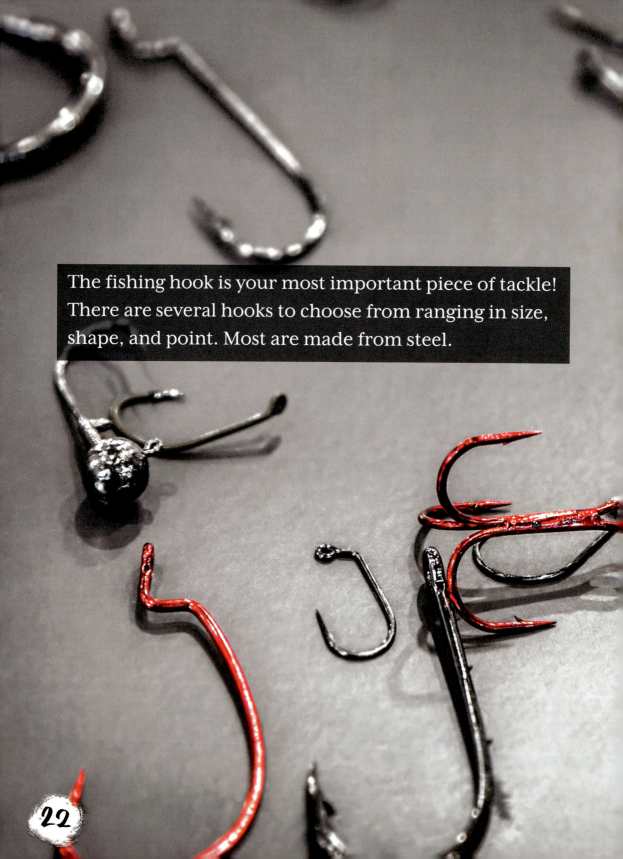

The fishing hook is your most important piece of tackle! There are several hooks to choose from ranging in size, shape, and point. Most are made from steel.

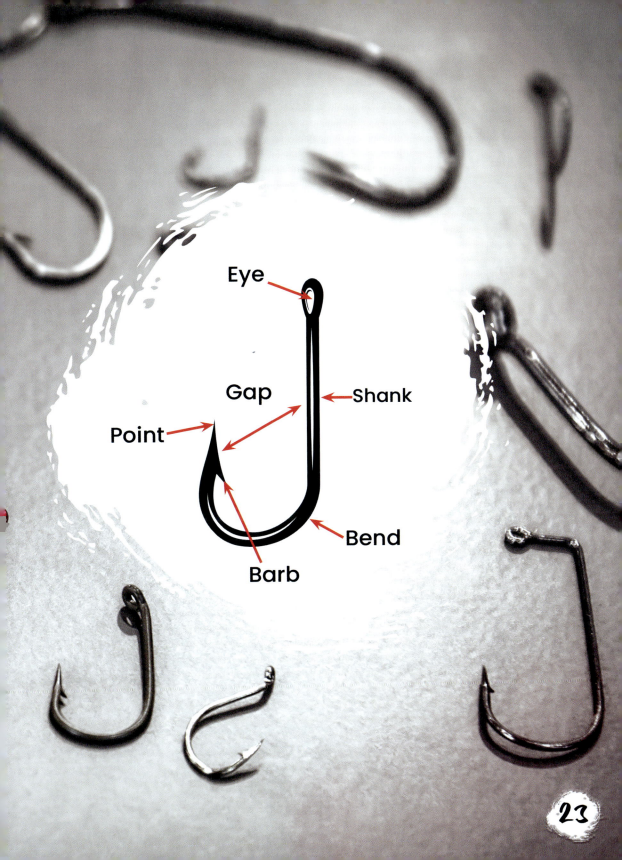

Eye

Gap

Point

Shank

Bend

Barb

You will need a pair of pliers to help get fish off your hook easily. You should also have a landing net to help secure your catch.

The cost of pliers is around $8 and a landing net is $20.

TYPES OF BAIT

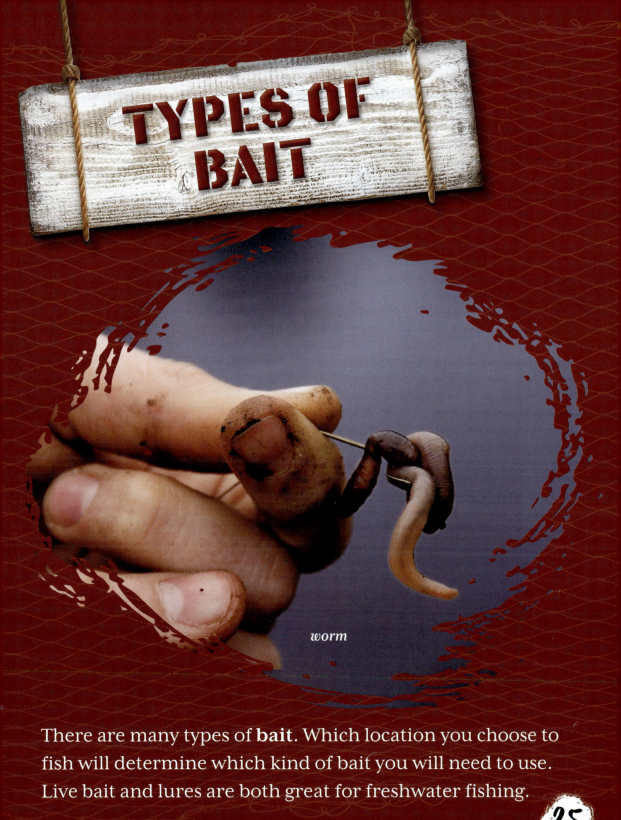

worm

There are many types of **bait**. Which location you choose to fish will determine which kind of bait you will need to use. Live bait and lures are both great for freshwater fishing.

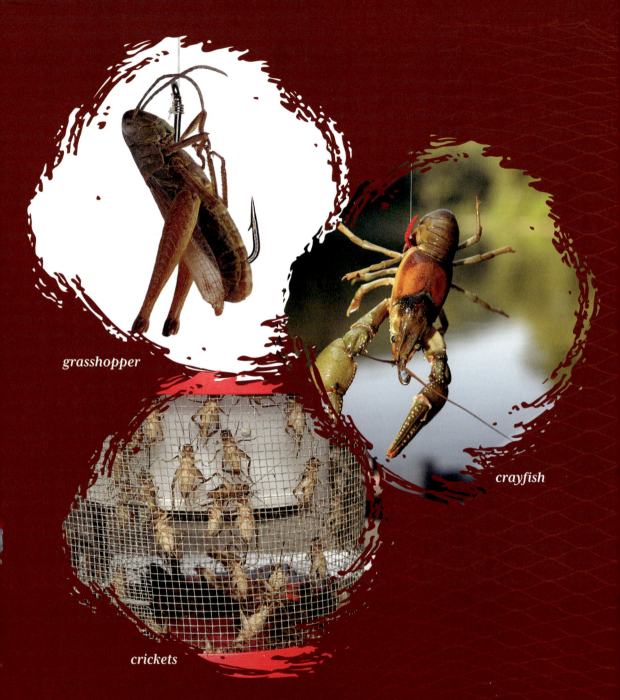

grasshopper

crayfish

crickets

Some live bait used in freshwater fishing are worms, leeches, minnows, crayfish, crickets, and grasshoppers. You can buy live bait or catch it yourself using a **cast net** or dip net.

Fishing lures come in all shapes, colors, and sizes. Jigs, poppers, spoons, plugs, and spinners are popular types of lures used. Each lure is designed to attract a certain type of fish.

Lures range in price from $6 to $25.

Freshwater fishing is fun. Fresh bodies of water are all around us. Grab a rod, tackle box, and bait, and go catch a fish!

FUN FACTS

Florida is considered the fishing capital of the world with around 3 million acres (1.2 million hectares) of lakes, ponds, and reservoirs and almost 12,000 miles (19,300 km) of fishable rivers, streams, and canals.

GLOSSARY

anadromous (uh-NAD-ruh-muhs): Traveling from the sea up freshwater rivers to breed

angler (ANG-gler): A person who fishes with a hook and line, especially for pleasure

bait (beyt): Food used to entice fish or other animals as prey

cast net (kast net): A net that is thrown out and then immediately drawn in again

fiberglass (FAHY-ber-glas): Fibers of glass used in making various products

largemouth bass (LAHRJ-mouth bas): A large North American bass of warm waters that is blackish green above and lighter or whitish below

license (LAHY-suhns): Permission granted by qualified authority to do something

lure (loor): An artificial bait used for catching fish

migrate (MAHY-greyt): To pass from one region or climate to another usually on a regular schedule for feeding or breeding

species (SPEE-sheez): A category of living things that ranks below genus

tackle (TAK-uhl): A set of special equipment

INDEX

WEBSITES TO VISIT

www.nationalgeographic.com/animals/fish/facts/freshwater-fish

www.takemefishing.org/freshwater-fishing/

www.fishingtipsdepot.com

ABOUT THE AUTHOR

Kerri Mazzarella was raised on the east coast of southern Florida. She has enjoyed fishing most of her life. Her family spends the weekends on their boat catching fish. All her teenage children are experienced anglers. Fish is often on the dinner menu at their house! Her favorite freshwater fish to catch is largemouth bass.

CRABTREE
Publishing Company

Written by: Kerri Mazzarella
Designed by: Kathy Walsh
Proofreader: Crystal Sikkens

Photographs: Shutterstock; Cover: ©Ryno Botha, ©MicroOne, ©Zerbor, ©GreyMoth; Pg 3, 4, 8, 12, 16, 20, 25 © ESB professional; Pg 1, 3, 8, 10, 13, 14, 16, 19, 25, 26 ©MicroOne; Pg 6, 10, 29 ©Zerbor; Pg 4 ©Ryno Botha; Pg 6 ©Slawomir Kruz; Pg 8 ©Fabien Monteil, ©Kletr; Pg 9 ©Harlan Schwartz, ©Pierre Rebollar; Pg 10 ©zsolt_uveges; Pg 11 ©Krasowit; Pg 12 ©gpointstudio, ©Mega Pixel, Pg 13 ©IRINA ORLOVA; Pg 14 ©Arne Beruldsen; Pg 15 ©Nadezda Murmakova; Pg 16 ©BigTunaOnline; Pg 17 ©BearFotos; Pg 18 ©Sergii Sobolevskyi; Pg 19 ©DoublePHOTO studio; Pg 20 ©ARENA Creative; Pg 21 ©nazarovsergey; Pg 22 ©OlegDoroshin; Pg 23 ©juligraphs; Pg 24 ©Kuznetcov_Konstantin; Pg 25 © jps; Pg 26 ©Edvard Ellric, ©Edvard Ellric, ©CLP Media; Pg 27 ©Petr Malyshev; Pg 28 ©New Africa

Library and Archives Canada
Cataloguing in Publication
CIP available at Library and Archives Canada

Library of Congress Cataloging-in-Publication Data
CIP available at Library of Congress

Crabtree Publishing Company

www.crabtreebooks.com   1-800-387-7650

Printed in the USA/072022/CG20220201

Published in the United States Crabtree Publishing
347 Fifth Avenue, Suite 1402-145
New York, NY, 10016

Published in Canada Crabtree Publishing
616 Welland Ave.
St. Catharines, Ontario L2M 5V6